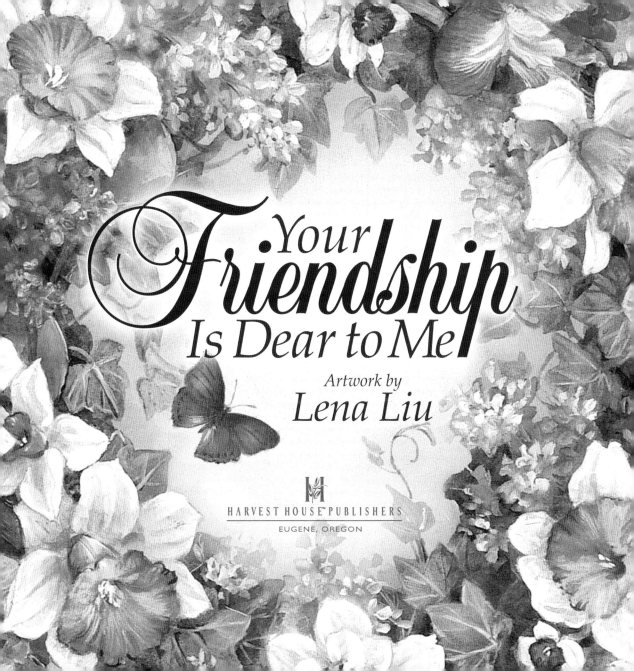

Your Friendship
Is Dear to Me

Artwork by
Lena Liu

HARVEST HOUSE™ PUBLISHERS

EUGENE, OREGON

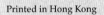

To My Dear Friend,

———————————————————————

With Love,

———————————————————————

A true friend is more precious

to the soul than all which it

inherits beneath the sun.

WASHINGTON IRVING

A little peaceful home bounds

all my wants and wishes;

Add to this my book and friend—

and this is happiness supreme.

Michel de Montaigne

Change, care, nor Time while life endure

Shall spoil our ancient friendship sure.

ANDREW LANG

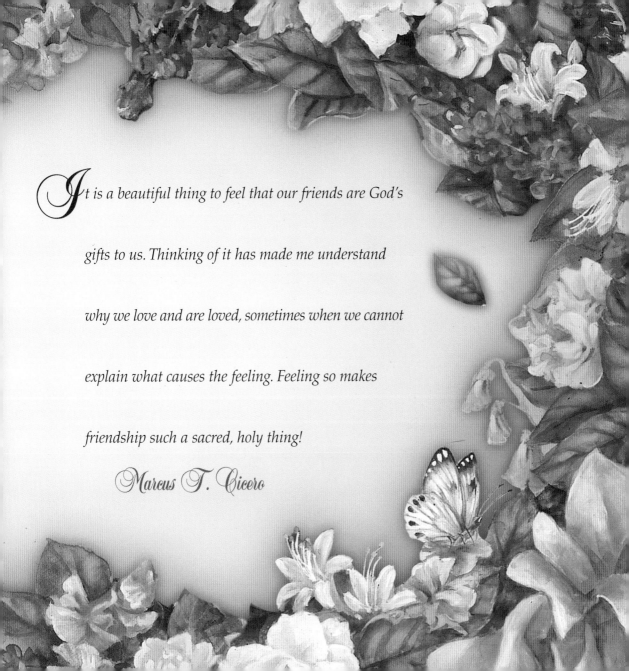

It is a beautiful thing to feel that our friends are God's

gifts to us. Thinking of it has made me understand

why we love and are loved, sometimes when we cannot

explain what causes the feeling. Feeling so makes

friendship such a sacred, holy thing!

Marcus T. Cicero

A principal fruit of friendship is the ease and discharge of the fullness and swelling of the heart, which passions of all kinds do cause and induce. No receipt openeth the heart but a true friend, to whom you may impart griefs, joys, fears, hopes, suspicions, counsels, and whatsoever lieth upon the heart to oppress it, in a kind of civil shrift or confession.

Sir Francis Bacon

Friendship is the holiest of gifts,
God can bestow nothing more sacred upon us!
It enhances every joy, mitigates every pain.
Everyone can have a friend
Who himself knows how to be a friend.

TEIDGE

Friendship hath the skill and observation of the best physician;

the diligence and vigilance of the best nurse;

and the tenderness and patience of the best mother.

Lord Clarendon

Old friends are the greatest blessings of one's later years.

HORACE WALPOLE

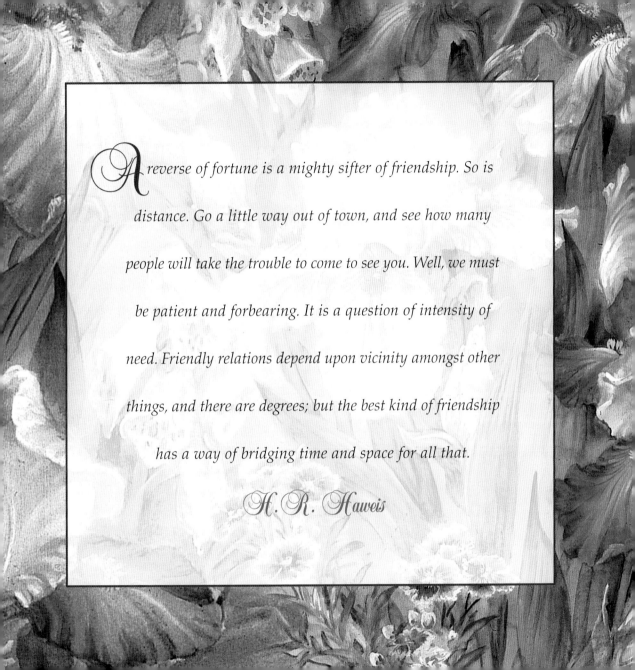

A reverse of fortune is a mighty sifter of friendship. So is distance. Go a little way out of town, and see how many people will take the trouble to come to see you. Well, we must be patient and forbearing. It is a question of intensity of need. Friendly relations depend upon vicinity amongst other things, and there are degrees; but the best kind of friendship has a way of bridging time and space for all that.

H. R. Haweis

Hearts are linked to hearts by God. The friend on whose fidelity you can count, whose success in life flushes your cheek with honest satisfaction, whose triumphant career you have traced and read with a heart throbbing almost as if it were a thing alive, for whose honor you would answer as for your own; that friend, given to you by circumstances over which you have no control, was God's own gift.

FREDERICK ROBERTSON

A true friend is forever a friend.

George MacDonald

After a certain age a new friend is a wonder.

There is the age of blossoms and sweet

budding green, the age of generous summer,

the autumn when the leaves drop,

and then winter shivering and bare.

WILLIAM THACKERAY

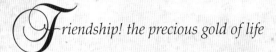

Friendship! the precious gold of life

By age refined, yet ever new;

Tried in the crucible of time

It always rings of service true.

Friendship! the beauteous soul of life

Which gladdens youth and strengthens age;

May it our hearts and lives entwine

Together on life's fleeting page.

J. Shaylor

A pure friendship inspires, cleanses,

expands, and strengthens the soul.

Horatio Alger

My friend, with you to live alone,

Were how much better than to own

A crown, a sceptre and a throne!

Alfred, Lord Tennyson

Believing hear, what you deserve to hear:

Your birthday, as my own, to me is dear.

Blest and distinguished days! which we should prize

The first, the kindest, bounty of the skies.

But yours gives most; for mine did only lend

Me to the world, yours gave to me a friend.

Marcus Valerius Martialis

Kindred passions and pursuits are the natural groundwork of

friendship. Real friendship is of slow growth, and never thrives,

unless ingrafted upon a stock of known and reciprocal merit.

PHILLIP CHESTERFIELD

LENA LIU

Such a friendship, that through it we love places and seasons; for as bright bodies emit rays at a distance, and flowers drop their sweet leaves on the ground around them, so friends impart favor even to the places where they dwell. With friends even poverty is pleasant. Words cannot express the joy which a friend imparts; they only can know who have experienced. A friend is dearer than the light of heaven, for it would be better for us that the sun were extinguished than that we should be without friends.

St. Chrysostom

Friendship, peculiar boon of Heaven,
The noble mind's delight and pride,
To men and angels only given,
To all the lower world denied.

SAMUEL JOHNSON

Even the utmost good-will and harmony and

practical kindness are not sufficient for friendship,

for friends do not live in harmony, merely, as

some say, but in melody. We do not wish for

friends to feed and clothe our bodies,—neighbors

are kind enough for that,—but to do the like

office to our spirits. For this, few are rich enough,

however well disposed they may be.

HENRY DAVID THOREAU

Friendship must live by faith and not by sight.

George Eliot

I want a warm and faithful friend,

To cheer the adverse hour;

Who ne'er to flatter will descend,

Nor bend the knee to power.

A friend to chide me when I'm wrong,

My inmost soul to see;

And that my friendship prove as strong

To him as his to me.

John Quincy Adams

Let Friendship's accents cheer our doubtful way,

And Love's pure planet lend its guiding ray,—

Our tardy Art shall wear an angel's wings,

And life shall lengthen with the joy it brings!

OLIVER WENDELL HOLMES

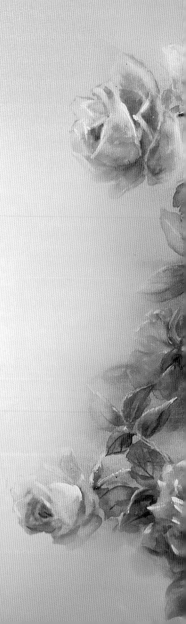

The highest compact we can make with

our fellow is, Let there be truth between us two forevermore.

It is sublime to feel and say of another, I need never meet,

or speak, or write to him; we need not reinforce ourselves

or send tokens of remembrance, I rely on him as on myself;

if he did thus or thus I know it was right.

RALPH WALDO EMERSON

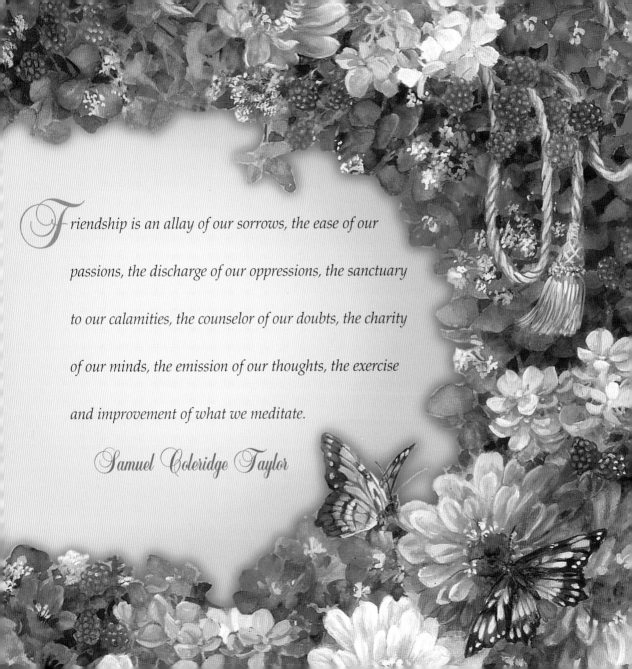

Friendship is an allay of our sorrows, the ease of our

passions, the discharge of our oppressions, the sanctuary

to our calamities, the counselor of our doubts, the charity

of our minds, the emission of our thoughts, the exercise

and improvement of what we meditate.

Samuel Coleridge Taylor

The mind never unbends itself so agreeably as in the conversation of a well-chosen friend. There is indeed no blessing of life that is any way comparable to the enjoyment of a discreet and virtuous friend. It eases and unloads the mind, clears and improves the understanding, engenders thoughts and knowledge, animates virtue and good resolutions, soothes and allays the passions, and finds employment for most of the vacant hours of life.

Joseph Addison

They who dare to ask anything of a friend, by their very request seem to imply that they would do anything for the sake of a friend.

Marcus T. Cicero

He has the substance of all bliss

To whom a virtuous friend is given:

So sweet harmonious friendship is,

Add but eternity, you'll make it heaven.

JOHN NORRIS

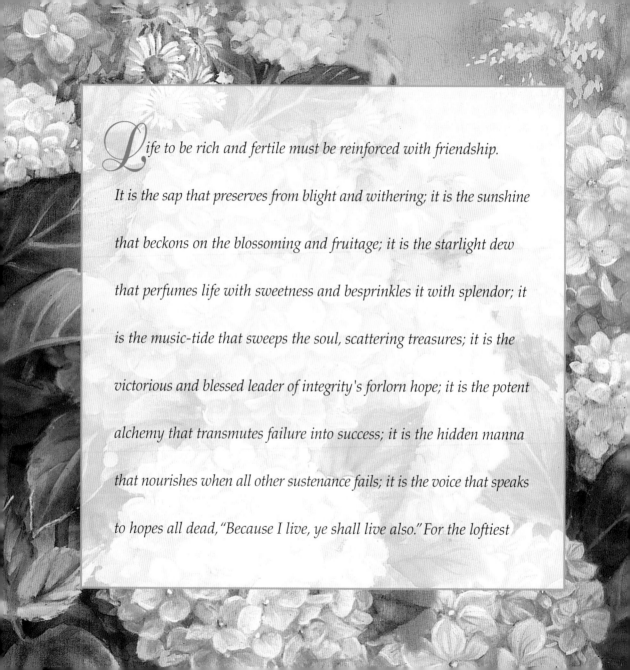

*L*ife to be rich and fertile must be reinforced with friendship.

It is the sap that preserves from blight and withering; it is the sunshine

that beckons on the blossoming and fruitage; it is the starlight dew

that perfumes life with sweetness and besprinkles it with splendor; it

is the music-tide that sweeps the soul, scattering treasures; it is the

victorious and blessed leader of integrity's forlorn hope; it is the potent

alchemy that transmutes failure into success; it is the hidden manna

that nourishes when all other sustenance fails; it is the voice that speaks

to hopes all dead, "Because I live, ye shall live also." For the loftiest

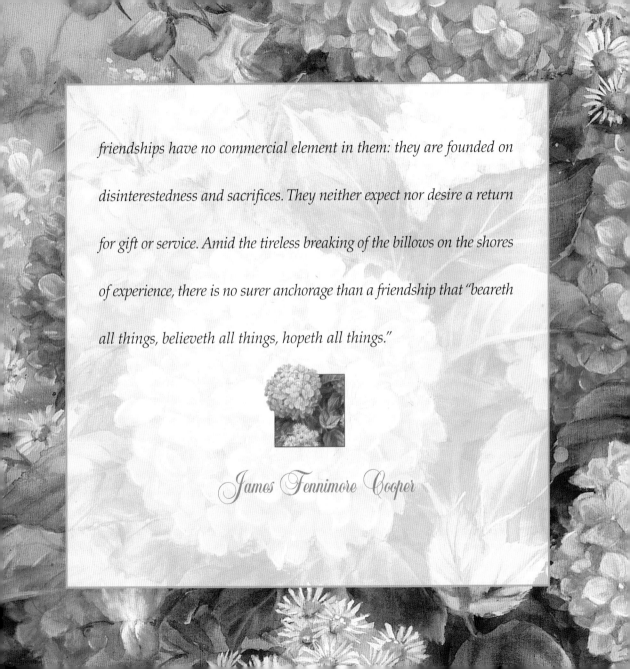

friendships have no commercial element in them: they are founded on

disinterestedness and sacrifices. They neither expect nor desire a return

for gift or service. Amid the tireless breaking of the billows on the shores

of experience, there is no surer anchorage than a friendship that "beareth

all things, believeth all things, hopeth all things."

James Fennimore Cooper

Thy friend will come to thee unsought,
With nothing can his love be bought,
His soul thine own will know at sight,
With him thy heart can speak outright.
Greet him nobly, love him well,
Show him where your best thoughts dwell,
Trust him greatly and for aye;
A true friend comes but once your way.

Author Unknown

Friendship consists in forgetting what one gives,

and remembering what one receives.

Alexandre Dumas

Blessed are they who have the gift of making friends, for it is one of God's

best gifts. It involves many things, but, above all, the power of going out of

one's self and seeing and appreciating whatever is noble and loving in another.

Thomas Hughes

And thou, my friend, whose gentle love

Yet thrills my bosom's chords,

How much thy friendship was above

Description's power of words.

Lord Byron

Friendship is steady and peaceful; not much jealousy, and no

heartburnings. It strengthens with time, and survives the

smallpox and a wooden leg. It doubles our joys, divides our

griefs, and warms our lives with a steady flame.

CHARLES READE

God never loved me in so sweet a way before;

'Tis He alone who can such blessings send;

And when His love would new expression find

He brought thee to me and He said, "Behold a friend."

AUTHOR UNKNOWN